AF882364

What Our Readers Have Said...

"The Pinpoint Training Series delivers information that could be used in a lot different areas."

•

"Applicable and valid. The information is good."

•

"I like this because I can take them with me to read at a convenient time. I feel the little time I have to spend in the office is best use on activities that directly relate to revenue opportunities. I like the short amount of time it takes to keep up with these."

•

"I like the fact that the format allows the books to be reviewed as time permits. All work has been conducted on personal, evening/weekend time."

•

"My thought is that the real value of these books comes into effect when doing the action plans."

•

"The challenge when I think a specific topic does not apply is to find a way to make it apply."

•

"Short and sweet. These books are easy to comprehend."

•

"These books are very easy to read and clearly outlined."

•

"I have enjoyed reading these books. They are relevant to today's work environment and the ongoing change in the way we manage our workforce."

•

"I believe the contents of the Pinpoint series are excellent. It causes one to reflect on the daily dynamics in working with oneself as well as with management and peers."

•

"Most of the information in these would help an open-minded management person, or an inexperienced management person."

•

"These books will pay for the time that I am investing. There are numerous good ideas that will streamline what I do and how I do it."

•

"All and all I think the Pinpoint series is a good program. I know other people I would love to have something like this. I think a lot of the suggestions are very useful, and can be applicable to everyday situations. If nothing else it's a good reference guide to fall back upon if a situation arises in the future."

•

"These books reinforce many concepts that I have learned through seminars, schooling and other programs. For myself, it serves as a constant learning tool that keeps me on top of the issues that many of us encounter every day."

•

"All in all, I think you have good training books. It helps everyone to review these materials, it serves as a good reminder to us on how to conduct ourselves."

•

"The information is valuable in these books."

•

Establishing Performance Standards for Sales Teams

Pinpoint Sales Management Skill Development Training Series

TIMOTHY F. BEDNARZ

MAJORIUM
BUSINESS PRESS

Pinpoint Sales Management Skill Development Training Series
"Establishing Performance Standards for Sales Teams"
Timothy F. Bednarz

Graphic design: Monika Pawlak

Majorium Business Press
2025 Main Street
Stevens Point, WI 54481
715.342.1018 • 800.654.4935

Copyright © 2011 Timothy F. Bednarz, Ph.D. All rights reserved. No part of this publication may be reproduced, distributed or transmitted in any form or by any means, including photocopying, recording, or other electronic or mechanical methods, without author's written permission.

ISBN 978-1-882181-64-3

Printed in the United States of America

Introduction

The Pinpoint Sales Management Skill Development Training Series is designed for targeted training and education regarding increased improvement in a specific skill or competency.

Each book within this series is designed to be easy to use, understand and apply to your job. It can be used as a basis for training individuals, as a discussion guide or as a personal training tool.

Each chapter within this book discusses a specific concept. When you have completed all eight chapters you should have a 360° perspective of the topic.

Additionally, each chapter is divided into specific sections:

- The first section provides you with an overview of the topic
- The Implications section discusses why the concept is important, and why it is important to learn and apply.
- The Strategies, Tips & Techniques to Apply section teaches how to use and apply the particular concept to your work.
- The Points to Ponder section gives you something to think about or to be discussed with a group setting. These are questions not meant to be immediately answered, but to be pondered over time.
- The Training Activity section provides you with the tools to transfer what you have learned to your job. It is designed to help create an action plan to effectively apply the concept.

Each of the topics in this series is time-tested and proven in the marketplace. They have been used by thousands of employees as training tools. Many of the users have commented that what made these books valuable, was the ability to refer to them when a problem surfaced. They indicated that they remembered reading about the exact problem. They referred back to these books and found an appropriate solution.

You will find them equally valuable as a resource in your professional development library.

Table of Contents

LEARNING OBJECTIVES:

- To understand the importance of performance standards.
- To establish performance standards for their salespeople and themselves.
- To evaluate the performance of their salespeople and themselves.
- To apply effective performance management skills and techniques.

1

Defining the Sales Manager's Responsibilities

Sales managers often have different ideas about where to focus their responsibilities. Many are deeply involved with their salespeople and daily activities to build sales, provide support and fill in any gaps. However, this is often completely at odds with what their primary responsibilities should be. Effective sales managers are more strategic than tactical, but many are former salespeople, and they understandably enjoy working in the field with prospects and customers. While to many sales managers this particular focus may seem like the most productive use of their time, it is actually detrimental to the performance of the department.

IMPLICATIONS — WHAT THIS MEANS TO YOU

Sales managers are often too caught up in a frenzy of daily activities and problems to stay focused on their primary responsibilities. Good management practices require sales managers to remain focused on attaining the overall goals and objectives of their sales team.

If sales managers want to become more effective and productive, they must concentrate their efforts on being more strategic and less tactical. This means delegating and supervising so that subordinates can manage the brunt of daily activities while sales managers focus most of their own time and energy on making progress toward larger goals. Sales managers provide guidance and direction, allowing others to deal with daily tasks that can often be distracting and time-consuming.

STRATEGIES, TIPS & TECHNIQUES TO APPLY

The primary role of the sales manager is to drive the performance of their sales team and increase overall results. The Professional Society of Sales and Marketing Training has prescribed five specific steps for accomplishing these goals. These key steps have been proven effective, as they concisely define the tasks and responsibilities sales managers must be cognizant of to successfully perform the job. These five key steps are:

1. Setting Objectives

During the performance management process, sales managers must set objectives for:

- Annual sales
- Business growth
- Professional growth

Individual and organizational objectives must be established at the same time in order to be effective and valuable. In this manner, what benefits the company also benefits the salesperson. The result is that the organization and the salesperson are working toward a common goal. The key is to focus everyone's energy on the same end point.

2. General Action Planning

Sales managers must work with their people to assure that performance objectives are fully implemented. Experienced managers determine the most effective methods for each salesperson to reach mutually acceptable performance standards. These standards allow sales teams and individuals to measure their progress at key points in the process, such as:

- Making sales calls
- Identifying and seeking decision makers

- Making sales presentations
- Closing sales
- Cold calling

General action plans allow sales managers to determine what individual salespeople are doing correctly and to pinpoint problem areas that need correction. This step is key to making the sales manager's job easier and more productive.

When establishing mutually acceptable goals, both the sales manager and salesperson must commit to objectives that are specific, measurable, realistic and timely.

3. Analyzing General Action Plans

When analyzing general action plans, sales managers must evaluate the individual strengths and weaknesses of each salesperson. Based upon this initial analysis, sales managers can develop training and job strategies that promote strengths and correct weaknesses. They must also include frequent feedback in this step.

The manager's observations of the individual salesperson are the basis for training, coaching and a fair evaluation of performance. The amount of time and effort that the sales manager will have to invest in each employee depends upon the individual.

4. Formal Evaluations

Sales managers must perform periodic formal evaluations of each salesperson that are frequent enough to provide an objective assessment of performance but not so frequent as to become an undue burden. These evaluations can be motivational tools that assist the sales manager and salesperson in setting future goals related to an individual's professional development and in defining new skills that need to be mastered to give him or her a competitive edge.

5. Renewing the Process

The responsibilities of the sales manager are never-ending. Once the previous four steps are complete, they must take time and care to renew the entire process, starting with revisiting the individual salesperson's goals and objectives.

Sales managers would do well in the process to keep four goals foremost in their minds:

- Reward excellence
- Remedy weaknesses
- Provide direction
- Generate enthusiasm

POINTS TO PONDER — SOMETHING TO THINK ABOUT

1. Do you feel that you are effectually moving your sales team forward?
2. What is the biggest source of frustration in your job as sales manager?

TRAINING ACTIVITY — APPLICATION & ACTION PLAN

1. Evaluate your performance as a sales manager. On a sheet of paper, create two columns. In the first column, list:
   - Setting Objectives (Strategic)
   - General Action Planning (Strategic)
   - Evaluating General Action Plans (Strategic)
   - Formal Evaluations (Strategic)
   - Renewing the Process (Strategic)
   - Sales & Selling (Tactical)
   - Sales Support (Tactical)
   - Customer Service and Support (Tactical)

2. In the second column, note the percentage of time that you devote to each respective activity.
3. Determine if you spend more time on strategic or tactical activities. Identify ways to focus on your primary responsibilities.

2

Monitoring Performance Using Sales Metrics

When employees are dealing with sales slumps and problems, it can create a tremendous drain on a sales manager's time and resources. The use of metrics that are linked to goals and objectives established in a salesperson's action plan can be an efficient and productive method of monitoring ongoing sales performance.

IMPLICATIONS – WHAT THIS MEANS TO YOU

With the aid of technology and a properly designed sales metrics system, managers should be able to adequately monitor the activities of their people without placing an undue burden on themselves. Sales managers have limited time and resources that can often be better utilized in other areas.

The best way to help struggling salespeople is to hold them accountable for their own activities and results. Sales metrics linked with defined goals and objectives give the sales manager the ability to effectively monitor a salesperson's progress without having to devote excessive time and energy. Metrics pinpoint problem areas, thus allowing sales managers to specifically target solutions. In this manner, time and resources are used with the greatest efficiency.

STRATEGIES, TIPS & TECHNIQUES TO APPLY

Sales managers who want to actively monitor the performance of slumping team members or want an established system of metrics for general measurement purposes should use the following steps:

1. Identify What Needs to Be Measured

The first step in the development of a sales metrics program is to determine the most important activities with which to measure a salesperson's progress against his or her goals.

Once an action plan and goals are established in collaboration with the individual salesperson, the manager should identify the specific areas that are appropriate and available to measure. All measurements should be quantifiable.

2. Identify Measurable Criteria

After sales managers have determined what needs to be monitored and measured, they should identify specific criteria. This will vary from person to person, but in general a sales manager might consider the number of calls, cold calls, proposals and orders a salesperson makes, as well as the dollar value of sales, unit sales, percentage increase in specific categories and return on investment.

3. Identify a Benchmark Standard for Performance

Managers will need to develop a benchmark standard for performance that can be used to evaluate the salesperson. It is often best to use the salesperson's past performance as an initial measuring standard, although the manager can certainly use an average of the entire sales team's performance as a benchmark. Also, people quite commonly employ a combination of measuring standards in their metrics.

4. Develop Reporting System

Once the measurement criteria and benchmarks are established, managers will need to determine how and with what frequency the data will be transmitted, collected and evaluated.

In certain cases, the data can be captured from the company's internal sales reporting system. In other instances, individual salespeople may be required to provide information in the form of sales summaries, call reports and other intelligence that gives the sales manager the vital metrics data.

Where possible, the collection and capturing of data should be automated to prevent unnecessary burden on the sales manager.

5. *Create Milestones*

Sales milestones should be determined as part of an action plan and metrics system. Milestones are specific performance levels that the salesperson is expected to achieve in a given period of time.

6. *Monitor Performance*

Once the metrics system is in place and operational, sales managers should actively monitor the individual's performance. A properly designed system will deliver a summary of key numbers and give the sales manager the ability to probe deeper into the report for specific details.

An effective system will also allow the sales manager to monitor activities at a glance, quickly assuring them the salesperson is following his or her own plan.

7. *Modify and Alter Based Upon Results*

As the salesperson works his or her plan, the manager can make alterations and modifications based upon reported results. A properly designed system should allow sales managers to anticipate problems and assist the salesperson before additional problems occur.

POINTS TO PONDER — SOMETHING TO THINK ABOUT

1. What measurement methods do you typically use to monitor the performance of your salespeople?
2. Have you used criteria that served as accurate predictors of future sales performance? What were they?

TRAINING ACTIVITY — APPLICATION & ACTION PLAN

1. Pinpoint the quantitative criteria that can be used to measure specific areas of performance.
2. Determine the significance of each criterion and establish where and when it should be used.
3. Identify benchmark standards.
4. Develop a sales metric "infrastructure" that can be easily modified in the process of monitoring and evaluating your salespeople.

3

Conducting a Sales Performance Audit

Sales performance audits (SPA) are a primary tool that sales managers use to analyze their organization, the selling environment and the members of their team.

In the face of increasing competition, volatile economic conditions and sophisticated customers and their demands, an SPA provides sales managers with an effective means of keeping pace with changes and controlling their sales team and its performance.

IMPLICATIONS – WHAT THIS MEANS TO YOU

Tools like SPAs are becoming more important for sales managers because they are an effective way to provide senior management with an overview of the sales organization and any potential performance problems.

Additionally, a SPA identifies steps that managers can take to increase sales while conducting a cost-benefit analysis of each decision.

These management tools are important to sales managers because they provide both the macro and micro views necessary to effectively manage sales teams.

STRATEGIES, TIPS & TECHNIQUES TO APPLY

A SPA should address senior management's concerns and expectations. Below are some key questions to consider.

Does the sales manager have a clear understanding of what salespeople should be doing?

Before sales managers can guide and direct the sales team, they must clearly understand what the primary roles and responsibilities are for each member. Selling is completely different from business development: one generates sales while the other builds business through established customer relationships.

Has the sales manager established clear goals and objectives that the average salesperson can understand and achieve?

Sales goals and objectives must be clearly and concisely defined in practical terms that salespeople can comprehend. If they do not understand what is expected, they cannot accomplish goals and objectives.

Moreover, salespeople must have goals and objectives that are achievable. Ambitious goals should be broken down into smaller, more easily achievable steps.

Does the sales manager structure assignments appropriately for the average salesperson?

The typical sales team includes salespeople with varying degrees of experience and expertise. Assignments should be structured to fit the background, experience and expertise of the individual. They should also be designed to always stretch the salesperson's abilities.

Does the sales manager train and coach salespeople when necessary?

Sales managers should consistently evaluate individual salespeople and help them polish existing skills and strengthen weak ones. By working to improve the skills of individuals, sales managers will ultimately enhance the overall performance of their sales team.

When sales support is needed, is the appropriate staff available to assist salespeople?

Nothing will destroy a sales team's productivity and motivation quicker than a lack of internal support. Salespeople deal firsthand with the needs of the customer. When a company fails to support the salesperson, they undermine their credibility with the customer.

When sales managers perform a SPA, they must start with an overview of their sales organization. This overview should summarize the goals and structure of the sales organization, all available resources, the sales environment, the sales skills and information required to effectively compete, the appropriate motivation and compensation, and the areas requiring management support.

The second phase of the SPA should review feedback from members of the sales team, to gauge their understanding of sales goals and responsibilities, individual performance reviews, and rewards and punishments for performance.

POINTS TO PONDER — SOMETHING TO THINK ABOUT

1. How deeply do you analyze the overall performance of your sales organization?
2. Do you meet the goals and expectations you set for yourself?

TRAINING ACTIVITY — APPLICATION & ACTION PLAN

Develop an SPA for your sales organization using the following criteria:

Organizational Analysis

- Product positioning

- Market segments
- Sales goals
- Plans and assignments
- Target accounts
- Key accounts
- Territories
- Customer information systems

Environmental Analysis

- Environment constraints
- Sales support
- Resources
- Sales tools and aids
- System access
- Feedback and consequences
- Incentives

Salespeople

- Sales skills
- Sales knowledge
- Sales motivation
- Personal attitudes

4

Pinpointing the Causes of a Sales Slump

It's obvious to a sales manager when a salesperson is in a slump. The plainest indicator is the lack of sales coming in from that individual. Less obvious are the causes of the slump, as they might be quite complex, not to mention masked by other circumstances and events.

IMPLICATIONS – WHAT THIS MEANS TO YOU

It is in everyone's interest to get salespeople out of a slump as quickly as possible. Not only is it important to the company for sales levels, productivity and performance to be restored, but if salespeople are not helped quickly, they will likely suffer long-term damage to their self-esteem and confidence that may be difficult to restore.

Personal attitudes and motivation are critical areas in selling. While sales slumps are natural, they cannot be allowed to damage the psyche of the salesperson. A loss of self-confidence can cause permanent damage to good salespeople to the point that they find it difficult, if not impossible, to restore their productivity. A loss of self-esteem can increase fears, anxiety and frustration, which will undoubtedly deepen the slump.

STRATEGIES, TIPS & TECHNIQUES TO APPLY

Sales managers need to examine several areas when trying to unearth the root causes of a slump. Often a slump can be complicated by a number of causes. In fact, sales managers may eliminate one cause only to see the slump recur because of other more complex causes. The elements outlined below can help managers identify the most common causes.

Sales Pipeline

Most sales slumps are triggered by an imbalance in the sales pipeline. In such instances, the salesperson has likely failed to sustain a pattern of prospecting and cold calling, leaving a lack of qualified prospects in the pipeline. At some point, they simply run out of prospects and must reinvest the time to start the whole process over. An immediate slump then occurs that can only be remedied over time as the salesperson brings new qualified prospects on board. The problem is that they will often repeat the cycle and end up in another slump after the new batch of prospects has filtered through the system.

Under these circumstances sales managers need to institute a sales metric system that measures all of a salesperson's activities. This system should have specific trigger points that alert the manager when specific sales activities drop below the prescribed and desired levels. Once alerted, sales managers can take immediate remedial action to prevent the salesperson from entering a full-fledged sales slump.

Economic and Market Conditions

As many companies know firsthand, dramatic shifts in market conditions and the resulting volatility can create immediate slumps that are out of the salesperson's control. It is difficult to sell a product when demand has effectively dried up.

Nevertheless, sales managers can attune themselves to trends in their market and industry that will impact their sales team. Shrinking demand and lengthening sales cycles can be anticipated. Sales managers who are aware of these signals can then shift their sales team's focus to other aspects of the business—such as the sale of service contracts and support services—to compensate for the downturn in overall demand.

Sales Skills

Dramatic shifts in economic and market conditions can expose poor sales skills. During boom times, overwhelming demand for a company's products and services can mask an individual's selling deficiencies. However, once demand dries up solid skills gain renewed importance. As a result, many salespeople flounder, especially those who never had to sell in volatile conditions.

Sales managers should take the time to observe their people at work in critical areas such as prospecting, cold calling, qualifying and closing. Managers should identify weaknesses and determine the appropriate course of action to rectify any problems. Some salespeople may require active training or coaching until their skills are honed.

Stress, Lack of Motivation and Burnout

Many salespeople have undoubtedly seen lucrative sales contracts vaporize in front of them during tough economic times. Many felt totally helpless in turning such situations around and consequently experienced high levels of stress that resulted in burnout and a lack of motivation.

Sales managers should monitor their salespeople for any dramatic changes in personality, such as increased frustration, loss of temper for minor reasons or a lack of concern over business affairs. Another key warning sign is complaints from associates and customers regarding the salesperson's behavior.

Sales managers who recognize these warning signs can counsel salespeople about their personal actions. However, sometimes salespeople require professional help to resolve deeper psychological problems associated with increased stress and burnout.

POINTS TO PONDER — SOMETHING TO THINK ABOUT

1. Can you identify or have you seen other symptoms of a sales slump?
2. Have you seen an increase in problems related to stress, burnout and lack of motivation during economic downturns?

TRAINING ACTIVITY — APPLICATION & ACTION PLAN

1. Examine current economic trends and leading indicators that relate to your industry.
2. Determine how you can steer your sales team around any potential problems and downturns you observe and thus move toward possible opportunities.

5

Performance Skills for the Sales Manager

Sales managers are under ongoing pressure to produce results for their companies regardless of economic and market conditions. This climate requires that sales managers possess a "toolbox" of proactive performance skills that allows them to adapt rather than react to shifting market and economic conditions.

IMPLICATIONS – WHAT THIS MEANS TO YOU

Sales managers must balance their performance according to five key areas of management. Sales managers are often most concerned about controlling and directing their sales team. But they must go beyond simply establishing quotas for individual salespeople. Effective planning and organization requires managers to set attainable goals and objectives that lead to sustainable growth. Selling is indeed a process with definable steps, and sales managers must establish standards for each step and use them to monitor each salesperson's performance.

Through effective monitoring of the sales process, progress can be evaluated and plans can be modified and adapted to reflect actual conditions in the marketplace. When sales managers rely primarily on sales quotas, they can only react after the fact.

STRATEGIES, TIPS & TECHNIQUES TO APPLY

Effective sales managers learn to master and balance the skills necessary to keep their teams performing at a high level. They focus their efforts on the areas discussed below.

Planning

Before they do anything else, sales managers must determine what they are responsible for accomplishing in their positions. The answer is partially informed by the goals and objectives of senior management and partially by the opportunities identified by both sales managers and members of the sales teams. Generally, sales managers want maximum use of all available resources, to ensure both productivity and profitability.

Planning must be comprehensive and ongoing. Plans need to be developed, monitored and adapted as economic and market conditions warrant. Managers cannot rely solely on annual reviews if they wish to maximize their sales teams' performance.

Organization

Once the scope of work and responsibilities has been identified, sales managers should divide the plan into manageable and attainable units. They must assign specific goals, objectives, tasks and responsibilities to their people that can be competently accomplished in a reasonable time frame. Within this framework, effective sales managers will harness their superior delegation skills, knowing who to assign specific goals and tasks to and how to work cooperatively with specific individuals.

Resource Development

Sales managers must ensure that they have the resources to accomplish their plans and achieve their goals. First and foremost, they need sufficient human resources. Effective sales managers interview, evaluate and hire individuals best able to work within the established plan.

However, simply hiring additional sales and support personnel is not sufficient. Sales managers must maximize individual performance by making sure that new employees are properly trained, coached and motivated.

Additionally, sales managers must ensure that they have other necessary resources, including office space, equipment, sales tools, promotional materials and product samples. Effective managers monitor resource procurement closely, as it can drain financial resources if not managed properly.

Leadership

Sales managers must be leaders. It is not sufficient for them to simply direct the sales team; they must maximize performance and ensure sustainable business growth by motivating, monitoring and coaching team members. Sales managers as leaders interact with their teams proactively to make certain that plans are implemented and goals are achieved. Part of a sales manager's responsibility includes identifying and understanding the strengths and weaknesses of each team member and aiding all in personal growth and development.

Management

Finally, sales managers are in fact obligated to focus some of their attention on the management and control of the sales team. In this role they create performance standards that they actively monitor and measure, taking corrective action when necessary.

While many will spend much of their time on this area, as they feel it is their primary charge, truly effective sales managers realize the importance of balancing their focus across all five areas. Consistent performance across the management spectrum comes with a dedicated investment of time and effort.

POINTS TO PONDER — SOMETHING TO THINK ABOUT

1. Do you feel your skills are balanced across all five areas of performance?
2. Can you think of other performance skills that may be required in your existing job?

TRAINING ACTIVITY — APPLICATION & ACTION PLAN

1. Across the top of a sheet of paper create six columns and label them thus: Skills; Planning; Organization; Resource Development; Leadership; Management.
2. In the first column, list all of the management skills you feel you possess (one skill per row). For each skill, place an X in any of the other five columns if you think the skill is important to that particular management area.
3. When finished, determine your areas of strength and weakness.
4. Based upon this assessment, develop a plan to strengthen your weaknesses.
5. Determine the extent of each weakness as well as what needs to be specifically done to overcome it.

6

Performance Management

Performance management allows sales managers to align the actions and activities of their sales teams with the goals and objectives of senior management in order to achieve the stated outcomes of the company.

This linkage provides sales team members with the practical basis to work toward the accomplishment of mutual goals and objectives.

IMPLICATIONS — WHAT THIS MEANS TO YOU

Many managers in an organization make the common mistake of assuming that because they understand the assigned goals and objectives, everyone else does. This assumption often causes sales managers to poorly handle or entirely miss performance problems. It can create a disconnect between established company goals and actual sales team activities. Salespeople who either did not hear or comprehend the communiqué will likely continue selling in a manner that is unrelated to newly established goals, thus assuring the failure of the larger company project.

Sales managers are critical components in the goal-achievement process because they are the liaison between management and the sales team. In many businesses, the goals of the company and the actions of salespeople lack any sort of connection. A results-oriented sales manager does everything in his or her power to align the daily activities of the sales team with the goals and objectives of the company.

STRATEGIES, TIPS & TECHNIQUES TO APPLY

Effective performance management always begins with sales managers. Before they can communicate the goals and objectives of senior management, they must clearly understand the desired ends and have a firm grasp on the means to those ends. Without a fully informed sales manager, a goal-achievement system can be plagued with gaps that ultimately cause faulty and incomplete results.

In many organizations, the problem stems from a lack of coherence between plans and results. It is quite common for sales managers and their people to develop annual sales plans and ignore them thereafter. Even when senior management mandates that these plans be crafted, they often lack connection to the daily reality of selling and thus are useless to people in the field.

Before sales managers can commit to performance management, they must personally pledge themselves to the process itself and ultimately to the achievement of results. Once done, they need to take the following steps:

1. Clarify Goals

Sales managers must take the time to create a dialogue with their sales team that begins by communicating the company's goals. Salespeople should be encouraged to question, challenge, interpret and clarify these goals. This step will allow them to gain ownership of the goal-setting process, which imparts personal meaning and increases the likelihood of the overall plan's success.

2. Discuss Ways to Meet Goals

Once salespeople understand company goals and objectives, sales managers should discuss specific ways the team can meet these goals.

These discussions should be detail-oriented so that sales strategies and plans can be carefully aligned with company goals. Salespeople must understand the precise changes they need to make in their individual selling behaviors, such as a shift in targets, selling styles, sales objectives and product mix.

Salespeople should clearly understand what management expects from them. Similar to the dialogue established in the goal-clarifying stage, salespeople should be encouraged to speak up to address concerns and brainstorm the best ways for achieving company goals and objectives.

3. Follow Through to Align Behaviors with Outcomes

The success of performance management hinges on the sales manager's commitment to following through with each individual salesperson to ensure that sales behaviors are aligned with desired outcomes. Unfortunately, many programs fall apart here: objectives and methodologies are discussed with the sales team (as in steps two and three), but individual salespeople eventually backslide into old sales habits that are misaligned with company goals.

Sales managers must harness the impetus to observe each salesperson's professional behavior, discuss with each individual the results they are seeing, and support and reinforce team efforts with additional training and coaching.

POINTS TO PONDER — SOMETHING TO THINK ABOUT

1. How proactive are you in the performance management of your sales team?
2. Are you personally committed to attaining company goals, or is it just "business as usual" for you?

TRAINING ACTIVITY — APPLICATION & ACTION PLAN

1. Assess your own sales team's alignment with company goals and objectives:
2. Determine if each salesperson understands the company's goals.
3. Identify if existing sales behaviors are well suited to achieve the goals.
4. Pinpoint any gaps between company goals and sales behaviors.

7

Developing a Performance Management Process

Sales managers are results-oriented individuals, and so are their salespeople. Most view reports and paperwork as hindrances to their performance rather than tools to maximize their output.

A good performance management program allows sales managers to align their team's objectives with the company's goals and to monitor individual performance.

IMPLICATIONS — WHAT THIS MEANS TO YOU

Many people in the business of sales dread planning and goal setting. When planning is done, it becomes little more than an endurance exercise—despite its potential to guide and direct their performance.

Performance management not only allows sales managers to align their sales team's performance with overall goals and objectives, but also gives them the management tools to assess an individual's performance and to keep salespeople focused and productive. In sum, it ensures maximum performance from the team.

STRATEGIES, TIPS & TECHNIQUES TO APPLY

The following steps should be followed to develop a well-defined performance management program for sales teams:

1. Establish Objectives

The establishment of performance management objectives is the key step in the development of a well-defined process. These objectives do not stand alone; they are closely linked to the company's strategic goals and objectives, and should clearly demonstrate how the sales team will take part in the company's plans. Objectives help align the desired output of the sales team with the company's financial goals, and they clearly define how the sales team will follow through during the year.

Sales managers provide their team with a roadmap that reveals the path for reaching the year's desired outcomes. Having completed that task, sales managers should be able to break the objectives down so each salesperson has a personal set of objectives that directly contribute to the attainment of the team's goals.

This first step clarifies the salesperson's direction and plainly shows how individuals truly contribute to the success of the company. Research has shown that when individuals are aware of how their work contributes to the company's success, they are more motivated and productive.

2. Develop Action Plans

Action plans show salespeople how to specifically accomplish their performance objectives. Experienced sales managers can help their sales teams determine the most effective ways for achieving individual performance objectives. In this manner, mutually agreeable standards of performance are established at key points. Action plans allow sales managers to easily determine what is going right or wrong, make modifications and keep individual salespeople focused.

3. Analysis

Sales managers must analyze their people's performance during the course of the year. The SMART method of analysis is the most adaptable way of observing, coaching and training. During this step sales managers and their teams agree to goals that are:

- Specific

- Measurable
- Attainable
- Realistic
- Timely

Individual performance is analyzed and adjusted based upon these mutually agreeable goals. The sales manager can use these criteria to specifically pinpoint problem areas and quickly correct them by adapting and modifying the action plan.

4. *Evaluation*

While most sales managers travel regularly with salespeople to discuss each one's performance, they should also establish time for formal evaluations. These evaluations should be frequent enough to give the sales manager an objective view of an individual's performance, but not so often as to cause an overburden of paperwork.

When sales managers establish standards for formal evaluations and spend an equal amount of time with each salesperson, they will have given equal consideration and direction to everyone on their teams. Sales managers should always be cognizant of the purpose of a formal review: to candidly assess what each salesperson has accomplished.

5. *Review and Renew*

The general purpose of a performance management program is to reward excellence, remedy weakness, provide direction and generate enthusiasm. To maintain the vitality of the program, sales managers should revisit goals and objectives at the end of each performance year.

At times new objectives will need to be established to realign the sales team with the company's goals. Once the review is complete and changes are made, a new one-year action plan should be developed for each salesperson.

Results-oriented sales managers will review and renew their plans at the end of each performance year. Effective performance management will help the sales team's success become directly linked to the accomplishment of company goals.

POINTS TO PONDER – SOMETHING TO THINK ABOUT

1. How closely are your sales team's objectives tied to company goals and objectives?
2. Do your salespeople understand how their personal performance is linked to overall company success?

TRAINING ACTIVITY – APPLICATION & ACTION PLAN

1. Using your organization's strategic plans, align your sales team's objectives with your company's goals.
2. Compare and contrast the new objectives with the sales team's existing objectives.

8

Keys to Performance Management

Effective performance management aligns all employees, not only the sales team, with the overall goals of the company. As a result, each employee understands their role in the organization (i.e., how their efforts contribute to its success) and strives to accomplish those goals.

IMPLICATIONS — WHAT THIS MEANS TO YOU

The sales manager has an important role to play in the formation of a performance management program for his or her sales team: company goals must be clarified and communicated and sales behaviors must be adjusted so that desired outcomes are achieved.

Properly implemented performance management demands time and patience. It also requires superior communication skills to close informational gaps that often exist between senior management's plans and the actual behaviors of salespeople on the job. Sales managers will find that once they close these gaps and clearly communicate the goals of the company to their salespeople, the program will work very efficiently, yielding a more productive sales team whose behaviors parallel organizational objectives.

STRATEGIES, TIPS & TECHNIQUES TO APPLY

The sales manager's responsibilities when it comes to performance management are to clearly communicate the company's goals, realign each salesperson's behavior and monitor performance. These responsibilities are further detailed below.

Clarify Goals

Research indicates that the performance of sales teams strongly depends on the level of clarity with which goals and objectives are communicated to them. When goals are clearly communicated, salespeople can focus on what needs to be achieved and how to achieve it. Simultaneously, all become unified in the accomplishment of these clear goals. On the other side of the coin, less clarity causes salespeople to focus more on personal goals to the detriment of team goals.

Limit Priorities

Many sales managers make the mistake of intermingling strategic goals with operational goals, or they have entirely too many priorities at the tops of their lists. These situations only blur the focus and lead to a lack of clarity. Sales managers are expected to narrow the focus of their priorities and limit their number to approximately five. They should also ensure that members of the sales team do the same. Too many priorities scatter the efforts of the sales team in an unmanageable variety of directions, which assures goals and outcomes will not be achieved.

Execution

Managers can expect good sales execution only when a salesperson's behavior is aligned with the company's goals. Many sales managers, however, don't know how to talk to employees about change and poor performance, and thus have problems getting salespeople on board with the company's direction. Also, some sales managers don't realize that successful execution will never happen without ongoing performance dialogue.

Most salespeople, once they understand how their sales goals fit into the overall company plan, will realize what they need to do to align themselves with these objectives and will then make the appropriate adjustments. However, without performance feedback from the sales manager, changes in execution will often fail.

Communicating Clearly

Quite often the only feedback salespeople receive during the sales year consists of how they are performing in relation to their stated sales goals; however, they need to be aware of the "bigger picture." Sales managers have the important responsibility of creating and elucidating linkages between the salesperson and the company so that individuals can see not only how they fit in but also how their efforts contribute to the company's success. Numerous studies have shown that when employees clearly understand their role in the organization and its success, they are more motivated and productive.

Sales managers should open up channels of communication with their salespeople to build a sense of community so that everyone can see how their efforts matter in the bigger picture of the organization.

Aligning Rewards with Goals

Sales managers must ensure that rewards encourage sales behaviors that are consistent with set goals, even if it means overhauling the sales compensation program. Most salespeople's behaviors are easily modified by a change in compensation: they will do whatever yields the most income.

Sales managers must be careful not to establish a performance management program without also reviewing their compensation program. If performance management is out of sync with compensation, the sales team will end up confused. Both programs must be closely aligned so that desired outcomes can be achieved.

POINTS TO PONDER — SOMETHING TO THINK ABOUT

1. Do you clearly understand your company's goals and their importance to the direction of your sales team?
2. Do you understand how you fit into your company's plans and contribute to its success?

TRAINING ACTIVITY — APPLICATION & ACTION PLAN

Develop a scenario for your sales team that demonstrates how they fit into the overall company plan and how their sales efforts contribute to everyone's success.

About the Author

Timothy F. Bednarz, Ph.D. is CEO of the American Management Development Group, Inc. For over 20 years he has researched, designed and authored hundreds of learning and development programs used by Fortune 1000 companies.

He is also the author of *Great! What Makes Leaders Great. What They Did, How They Did It and What You Can Learn from It* (2011).

Speaking Availability

Timothy F. Bednarz, Ph.D. is available for speaking engagements for your next meeting or association event. He can be contacted at 800-654-4935 or by e-mail at timothy.bednarz@majorium.com.

Bulk Sales

Bulk sales of this book or any other titles available from Majorium Business Press. Inquiries can be directed to sales@majorium.com, or by phone at 800-6654-4935.

Quick Order Form

Fax orders: 715-342-1118. Send this form.

Telephone orders: Call 800-654-4935 toll-free. Have your credit card ready.

Email orders: sales@majorium.com

Postal orders: Majorium Business Press, 2025 Main Street, Stevens Point, WI 54481, USA.

Please send the following books:

____

____

____

____

Please send more FREE information on:

❑Catalog ❑Speaking/Seminars ❑Mailing Lists ❑Consulting

Name: ____

Address: ____

City: ________________________ State: ____ Zip: ________

Telephone: _______________________________________

Email address: ____________________________________

Sales tax: Please add 5.5% for products shipped to Wisconsin addresses.

Shipping by air:

United States: $4.00 for first book and $2.00 for each additional product.

International: $9.00 for first book; $5.00 for each additional product (estimate).

Made in the USA
Monee, IL
04 November 2026

67377572R00026